THINGS OF VALUE:

NATURAL RESOURCES

IN THE USA

ENVIRONMENTAL ECONOMICS GRADE 3 | ECONOMICS

BIZ HUB
business | investing

First Edition, 2020

Published in the United States by Speedy Publishing LLC, 40 E Main Street, Newark, Delaware 19711 USA.

© 2020 Biz Hub Books, an imprint of Speedy Publishing LLC

Biz Hub Books are available at special discounts when purchased in bulk for industrial and sales-promotional use. For details contact our Special Sales Team at Speedy Publishing LLC, 40 E Main Street, Newark, Delaware 19711 USA. Telephone (888) 248-4521 Fax: (210) 519-4043. www.speedybookstore.com

10 9 8 7 6 * 5 4 3 2 1

Print Edition: 9781541953215
Digital Edition: 9781541956216

See the world in pictures. Build your knowledge in style.
www.speedypublishing.com

CONTENTS

In this book, we're going to talk about natural resources within the United States and within your particular state, so let's get right to it!

WHAT IS A NATURAL RESOURCE?

A natural resource is something that is part of the Earth or an animal or plant. For example, the soil we have on Earth is a natural resource.

One of Earth's natural resource, soil

The air and the water are natural resources too.

The wood from trees is a natural resource.

Fruits and vegetables are natural resources.

Animals we use for meat are
also natural resources.

All natural resources have value, but they don't all have value for the same reason. We can use them for food, shelter, clothing, or fuel. You can think of most natural resources as falling under the categories of animal, vegetable, or mineral.

An illustration of the environment and its natural resources

The animal and vegetable
categories are renewable resources,
but the mineral category is not.

12

Everywhere we look there are natural resources, but they're not distributed evenly all around the planet. For example, some areas have lots of water, but other areas have so little water that they have desert climates.

Desert in Wadi Rum, Jordan

Countries that have many natural resources, such as the United States, have an advantage over other countries.

UNITED STATES
ENERGY AND ECOLOGY INFOGRAPHICS

O_2

CO_2

H_2O

THERMAL		RENEWABLE ENERGY						
Nuclear	Thermal	Biomass	Osmosis	Solar	Wind	Hydroelectricity	Marine	Pumped storage

They can export their resources to other countries to obtain the things that they need. For example, countries that have large areas covered in forests generally export wood and paper products.

Woods and paper products for exporting

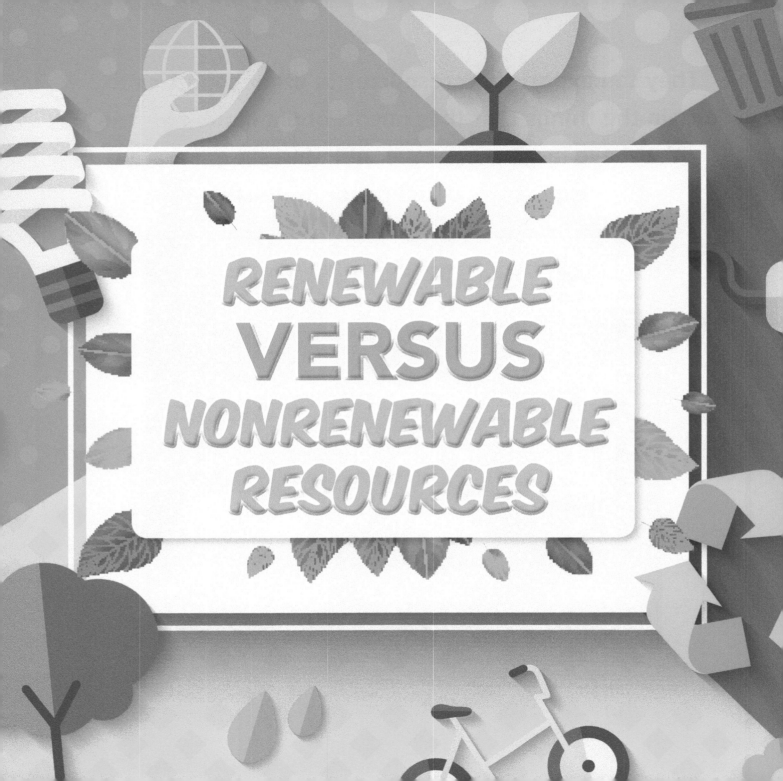

RENEWABLE VERSUS NONRENEWABLE RESOURCES

Harvest of timber

If a natural resource is used and there's some way to replace it, then it's called a renewable resource. Timber is an example of a resource that is renewable.

Man plants
a tree

Once a tree is cut down another tree can be planted to
replace it. It will take a while, but eventually that tree will
be grown and can be cut down for wood.

However, metals and fossil fuels that are mined from the ground are nonrenewable. These types of natural resources take millions of years to form so they are nonrenewable because they can't be replaced.

NATURAL
RESOURCES
IN THE UNITED
STATES

One of the primary industries in the United States is mining. The total reserves of both coal and metal are estimated at approximately $110 billion.

Aerial view of copper mining in Tucson, AZ

Compared to other countries around the world, the U.S. has been the top producer of coal for many years. About 30% of the world's coal comes from U.S. mines.

Coal Mine, Fairmont, West Virginia

Fairmont Coal Co. – Monongah Mine.

The United States also has enormous quantities of timber. It's estimated that the United States has over $45 trillion in natural resources. Ninety-percent of those resources are estimated to be made up of wood and coal.

A charcoal factory

Other significant resources include metals, such as gold and copper, as well as fossil fuels, such as crude oil and natural gas.

Gold

Copper

Emission from coal power plant

A skeleton of an
animal buried in
the ground

Energy sources that were formed from buried animals and plants that died millions of years in the past are called non renewable sources of energy.

Dead leaves

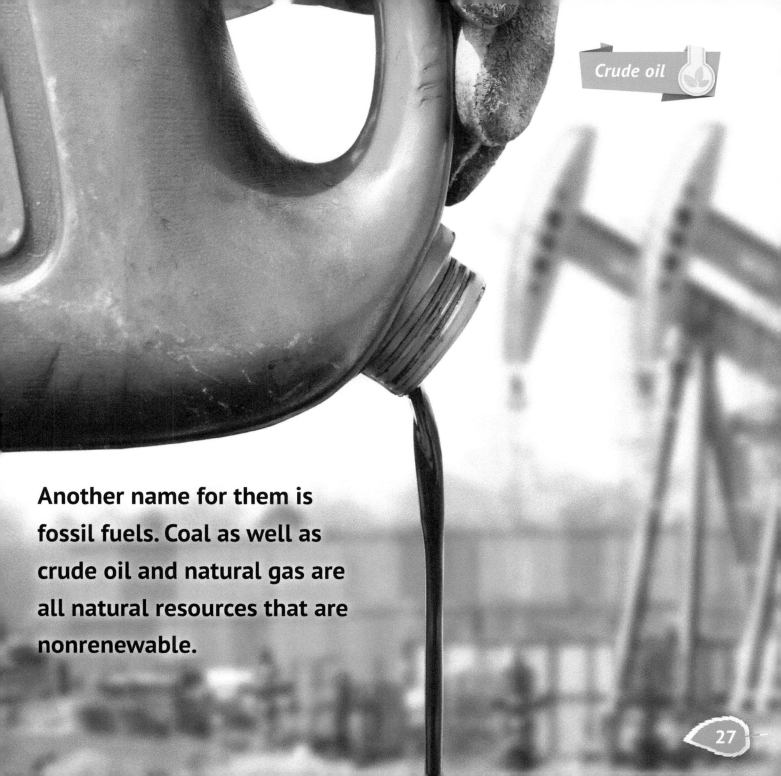

Another name for them is fossil fuels. Coal as well as crude oil and natural gas are all natural resources that are nonrenewable.

Crude oil, also known as petroleum, is a liquid.
Natural gas is most often in the form of a gas.
Coal occurs as solid lumps. All of these fossil
fuels are mined from underground.

Aerial view of tank farm for bulk petroleum and gasoline storage

All fossil fuels fall in the nonrenewable category. However, not all nonrenewable sources of energy are fossil fuels.

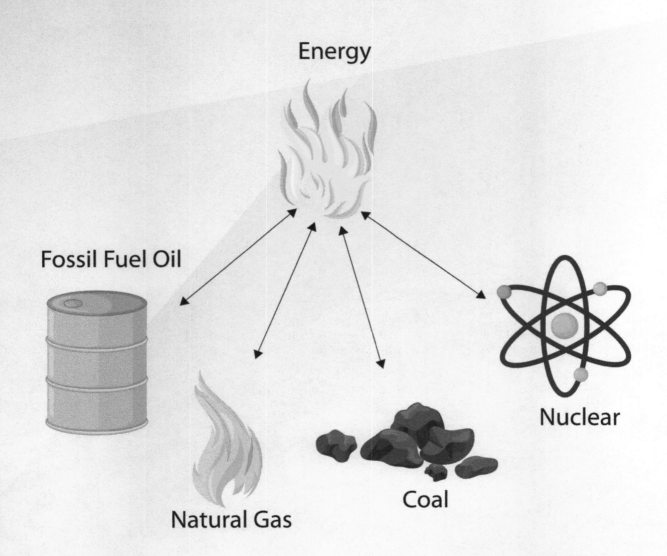

Energy

Fossil Fuel Oil

Natural Gas

Coal

Nuclear

For example, uranium ore is a natural resource that is not a fossil fuel. It is a solid and is mined as fuel for nuclear power plants.

Gummite (uranium ore) from Brasil

Thirty-one states produce crude oil, but over 60% of all crude oil comes from Texas, North Dakota, California, Alaska, and Oklahoma with more than half coming from Texas.

Oil drilling rig in the Texas

North Dakota Oil Pump

Alaska north slope drilling platform

Pump-jack, Oklahoma

Oil field in Bakersfiled, California

Crude oil is mined from underground and offshore wells. About 20% of all the crude oil mined in the United States comes from offshore wells located in the Gulf of Mexico.

Offshore oil and natural gas drilling platform in the Gulf of Mexico

Barrels of crude oil

Despite the abundant supplies of crude oil in the United States we still need more to run our vehicles and machines.

We import about 40% of the crude oil that we use from other countries.

The US still buys crude oil from other countries to run their machines

Natural gas is a nonrenewable resource. Natural gas is a vital component to many of the products we have in our homes, schools, and offices.

Infographic of methods of extracting natural gas

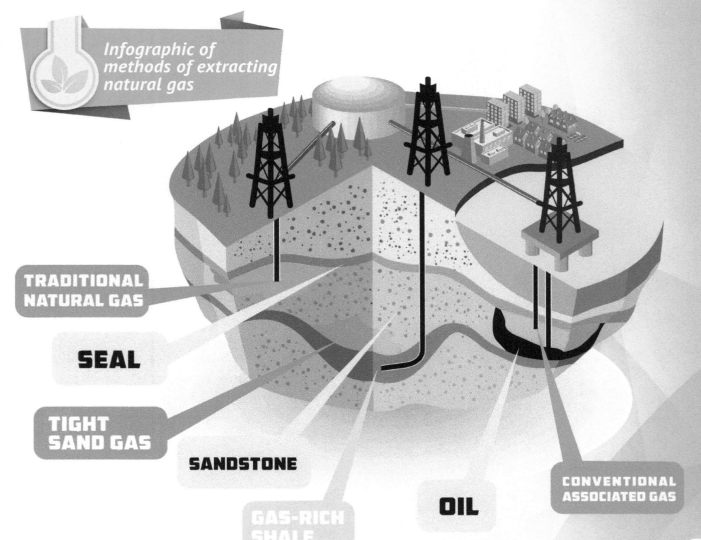

TRADITIONAL NATURAL GAS

SEAL

TIGHT SAND GAS

SANDSTONE

GAS-RICH SHALE

OIL

CONVENTIONAL ASSOCIATED GAS

It's used to make steel and glass as well as paper.

Glass blowing process

Without natural gas, there wouldn't be paints, plastics, films, fertilizer, or many types of medicines.

Paints

Plastic objects

Fertilizers

Film strip

Medicines

About half the homes in the United States also use natural gas to power household appliances such as stoves, dryers, and heaters.

Natural gas used at home for cooking

Through 1986, the United States was supplying most of the natural gas that was needed to meet the demands of households and businesses.

In the past, the US was able to supply most of its needed natural gas

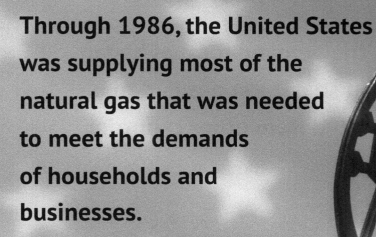

However, after that, the demand for fuel began to outpace production so natural gas had to be imported from other countries.

Natural gas storage tanks

To meet this demand without the need for imports, new, cost-efficient drilling techniques were invented to get natural gas from shale, which is a type of rock formation.

Well is turned horizontal

Shale

An illustration of Shale drill rig

Hydrofrack zone

45

From the years 2006 to 2011 production increased. The states of Texas, Louisiana, and Wyoming produce the most natural gas. The Federal offshore section of the Gulf of Mexico and the state of Oklahoma are top producers too.

Natural gas rig in Galveston Bay, Texas

Liquefied natural gas plant in Louisiana

Oil drilling rigs in the oil fields of Wyoming

Aerial view of offshore oil platform, Gulf of Mexico

A natural gas transfer and storage facility on the plains of Oklahoma

Despite the new, more efficient methods of extracting natural gas, the United States still has to import about 6% of its natural gas to meet the demands. About one-fourth of all the energy used in the United States comes from natural gas.

Coal is a fossil fuel that took millions of years to form from dead plants that lived when the Earth had a very swampy environment.

Multiple Coal Fossil Fuel Power Plant

Coal is mined from the Earth and is grouped into different categories. The coal closest to the surface has the most water content.

Open pit mine,
extractive industry
for coal

51

Coal from mines

The types that are deeper have been under massive amounts of pressure for millions of years. They have the most carbon and the least water. Those with the most carbon also produce the highest heat.

There are four main types of coal. This list is organized by the closest to the Earth's surface down to the deepest coal found.

- **Lignite**
- **Sub-bituminous**
- **Bituminous**
- **Anthracite**

Lignite, also called brown coal, is the wettest type of coal. It also has the least carbon so it gives the lowest amount of heat.

Lignite

Sub-bituminous is a dark brown to black coal, which ranks between lignite and bituminous coal.

Bituminous or soft coal is used a lot for fuel because it gives a lot of heat and exists in large amounts. Its disadvantage is it contains a lot of sulfur.

Bituminous

Anthracite is a very desirable fuel. It gives high heat, but doesn't contain much sulfur. However, its supply is limited in most locations.

Anthracite

In the United States, coal is mined in three main coal regions:

- **The Appalachian**
- **The Interior**
- **The Western**

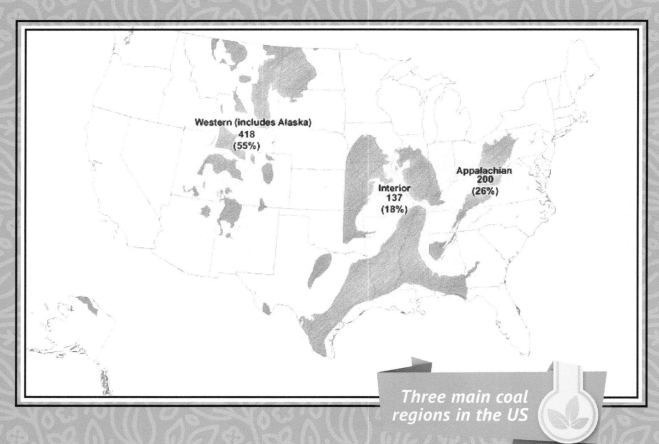

Three main coal regions in the US

The Appalachian coal mines produce about 29% of the nation's coal. West Virginia produces the most and ranks second only to Wyoming.

Aerial view of a coal mine in West Virginia

The coal mined here is used to create electricity. It's also exported to other countries.

Rail cars loaded with coal from nearby mines to power plants in Wyoming

Illinois is the state that produces the most coal in the Interior region. It produces about 27% of all the coal mined there.

Coal mining in Illinois

Over 50% of all coal mined in the U.S. comes from the Western coal region. The largest coal producer in this region is Wyoming and it's also the largest coal producing state.

Coal mine, Gillette, Wyoming

63

Ninety percent of the top-producing mines are located in this region and they are some of the largest mines in the world.

Coal haul truck at the North Antelope Rochelle opencut coal mine, Wyoming

Most of the coal mined in the United States, about 93%, is used to create electricity. The remaining coal is used in the manufacturing of steel, paper, and cement.

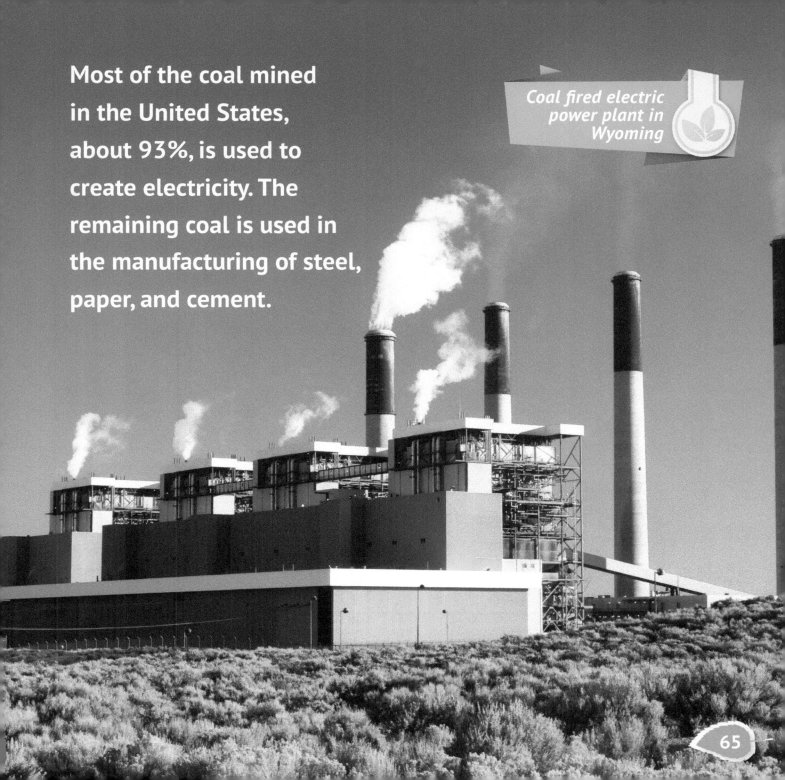

Coal fired electric power plant in Wyoming

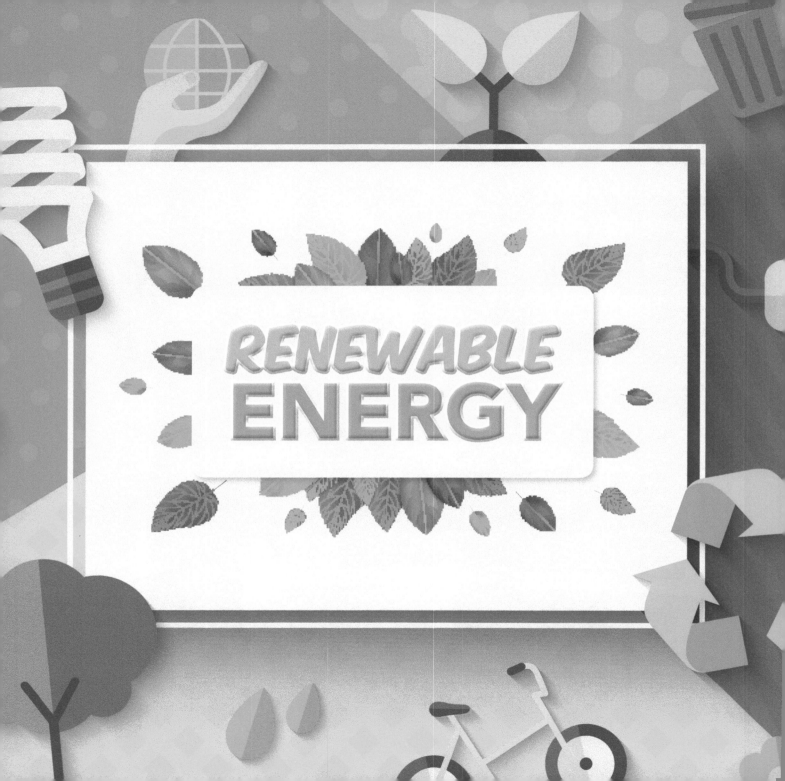

The United States also produces renewable energy from natural resources such as sunlight, wind, and water. For example, California is the state that produces the most solar power directly from sunlight, a renewable natural resource.

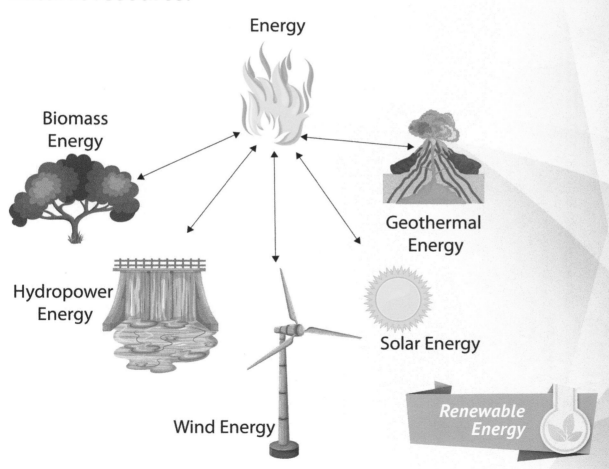

Energy

Biomass Energy

Geothermal Energy

Hydropower Energy

Solar Energy

Wind Energy

Renewable Energy

Iowa, North Dakota, and California are all leaders in wind power.

Iowa

California

North Dakota

The best way to quickly discover your state's specific animal, vegetable, and mineral natural resources is by studying a natural resource map. You can find these maps by looking through a detailed United States atlas. A resource map has icons that show natural resources from crops to livestock to minerals.

United States Natural Resources map

For example, the state of
Florida produces a large
quantity of the world's oranges.

*Rows of Orange
Groves. Florida
Agriculture*

The state of Texas has many ranches that produce high-quality beef. Texas is also known for its oil and minerals.

Cowboy in Texas gathering Texas Longhorn

The state of Kansas is known for its wheat and corn production.

Kansas wheat and corm

Potatoes are identified with the state of Idaho and Vermont is known for its dairy farms.

Idaho potato farm and dairy cows in Vermont

NATURAL RESOURCES IMPACT THE SELECTION OF BUSINESSES

Many businesses in a particular state thrive there because the natural resources they need are there in abundance. For example, if you wanted to start a business manufacturing products made from apples, the state of Washington in the northwest would be a great location.

Washington Apples harvested every fall season

Sixty-five percent of the apples grown in the United States come from Washington, followed by the state of New York.

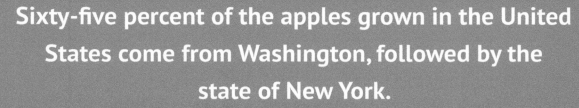

Rows of blossoming apple trees in Washington State's Wenatchee Valley

WHY A CLEAN ENVIRONMENT IS IMPORTANT

We need the natural resources on Earth to survive and thrive. That's why it's important for us to keep our environment clean and free from pollutants.

An illustration of a clean and healthy environment

When the air, water, and land are polluted it affects all the animals and plants on Earth because all natural resources are connected.

The United States is abundant in natural resources. Worldwide, it is a top producer of coal, a nonrenewable resource, as well as timber, a renewable resource. Natural resources in each state can be categorized as animal, vegetable, and mineral. One of the best ways to find out the top natural resources in your state is to use a United States atlas. In an atlas, there are special maps that have icons showing the top resources in your state. Some of these maps highlight areas of the state where the production of particular resources is highest. Everything in our environment is a natural resource. In order for us to grow healthy crops and livestock, the air, land, and water, which are also natural resources, must be free of pollution.

Awesome! Now that you've learned about natural resources within the United States and within your state, you may want to read more about other aspects of economics in the Baby Professor book, *Economics for Kids - Understanding the Basics of An Economy | Economics 101 for Children | 3rd Grade Social Studies.*

Visit

www.BabyProfessorBooks.com
to download Free Baby Professor eBooks and view our
catalog of new and exciting Children's Books

Lightning Source UK Ltd.
Milton Keynes UK
UKHW050956010520
362622UK00002B/54